TRUE CRIME

FORENSICS

T. R. Thomas

SADDLEBACK
EDUCATIONAL PUBLISHING

TRUE CRIME

SADDLEBACK
EDUCATIONAL PUBLISHING

www.sdlback.com

ISBN-13: 978-1-59905-439-1
ISBN-10: 1-59905-439-6
eBook: 978-1-60291-765-1

15 14 13 12 11   1 2 3 4 5

Photos:
Walter Dandridge, Brooks Kraft/Corbis
Lori Drew, Ted Soqui/Corbis
John List, Kathleen W. Perlett/Star Ledger/Corbis

CONTENTS

INTRODUCTION

Forensics is the use of science to help solve crimes. It can also be used in other legal arenas.

Forensics was used in ancient Greece. Archimedes used forensics to prove that a royal crown was not solid gold. It was too light to be pure gold.

Today forensics is a highly advanced science. There are many different branches.

Forensic dentistry, or *odontology*, looks at teeth. Bite mark analysis can help determine who committed a crime. Dental records can also help identify victims.

5

FORENSICS

Ballistics is the study of guns and bullets. *Forensic ballistics* can show which gun was used in a crime.

In *computer forensics*, scientists study computers. They can look into a killer's computer. They can tell when emails were sent and to whom.

Facial reconstruction shows what a dead person's face looked like. Scientists use the victim's skull. They make a drawing, a clay model, or a computer likeness of the face.

Fingerprinting is one of the oldest forensic sciences. It was used as early as the 7th century. Each person's fingerprints are unique. Fingerprinting is very helpful in solving crimes.

Forensics has come a long way since Archimedes' time. Today police use forensics to solve even the most complex crimes.

CHAPTER 1

FORENSIC DENTISTRY

DATAFILE

T I M E L I N E

March 1850

Dental evidence is first used in a U.S. court to identify a body.

February 16, 1972

The Vampire Rapist, a Canadian serial killer, is sent to prison.

July 29, 1994

Megan Kanka, age 7, bites her attacker's hand. The bite helps convict her murderer.

Where is Montreal, Quebec, Canada?

KEY TERMS

controversy—an issue people disagree on

interpret—to explain the meaning of something

odontology—the study of teeth and gums

orthodontist—a type of dentist who fixes crooked teeth

subjective—based on opinion rather than fact

DID YOU KNOW?

In 2005, Ray Krone was on the TV show *Extreme Makeover*. Krone used to be known as the Snaggletooth Killer. He was proven innocent in 2001. The show replaced five of his front teeth as part of his makeover.

FORENSIC DENTISTRY

In October 1969, Canadian police found a young woman's body. It had been dumped behind some apartments. Shirley Audette, 20, had been murdered. There were bite marks on her body.

Her killer, Wayne Boden, later became known as the Vampire Rapist. He raped and killed four women in Montreal. He savagely bit them during the attacks. Then he moved nearly 2,000 miles away to Calgary. He attacked another woman there. Police caught him shortly after that.

Canadian police asked *orthodontist* Gordon Swann for help. Swann contacted the U.S. FBI for advice. He then made a cast of Boden's teeth. Investigators compared the cast to the Calgary victim's bite wounds. There were 29 points of similarity. It was enough to convict.

The Vampire Rapist's bites put him away for good. Wayne Boden was the first murderer ever convicted by bite mark evidence. The year was 1972. Boden died in prison in 2006.

Forensic Odontology

Forensic dentistry is the study of teeth to solve crimes. It is also known as forensic *odontology*. Forensic dentistry has two main uses. One is to identify bodies using dental records. The other is to use bite mark evidence to convict criminals.

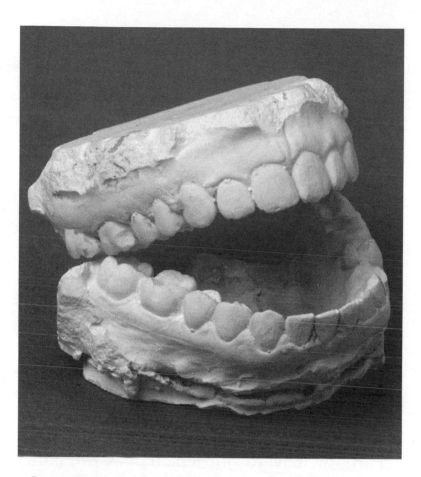

Investigators, comparing a cast of Boden's teeth to the victim's bite wounds, were able to prove that he was the Vampire Rapist.

Sometimes a victim's body is badly burned or otherwise unrecognizable. In these cases, scientists may look at the victim's teeth. They are compared to dental records. The victim can be identified that way.

False Teeth Hang a Murderer

Forensic dentistry was first used in a U.S. court in 1850. A sensational trial took place in Boston. A wealthy man named George Parkman had been murdered. Dr. Nathan Keep was his dentist. He had made false teeth for Parkman.

The killer cut up Parkman's body. Parts of it were burned. It was difficult to prove it was even him. However, a jawbone was found. It contained the false teeth. Dr. Keep recognized his work. He told the court he was sure the body was Parkman's. Dr. Keep's statement helped convict Professor John Webster. He was hanged for murder.

Tidal Wave!

Forensic dentistry is also used after mass disasters. It's hard to identify victims when there are many bodies. That's where forensic odontology comes in.

A tsunami struck southeast Asia in 2004. The huge tidal wave killed more than 200,000 people. Dental records helped identify the bodies. Some victims had never been to a dentist. Many of these bodies remain unidentified even today.

Bite Marks Can Prove Guilt

Bite mark evidence is another important use of forensic dentistry. Wayne Boden was the first murderer convicted by this type of evidence. Infamous serial killer Ted Bundy was another. Bundy killed at least 29 young women. He may have killed more than 100. He killed so many he lost count.

Bundy was good at covering up his crimes. But his bite gave him away. One of his last victims was Lisa Levy. She was a college student in Florida. Bundy attacked her in her bed one night. He bit her during the attack. The bite marks on her body matched Bundy's teeth. This and other evidence convicted him. Ted Bundy was executed in Florida in 1989.

Megan's Law

Bite mark evidence was also crucial in the Megan Kanka case. The little girl, age 7, had been murdered. She bit the killer's hand as he was attacking her. Megan's bite marks helped convict Jesse Timmendequas. He had lived across the street from the Kankas.

Timmendequas was a violent sex offender. He'd been in prison. But people in the neighborhood didn't know. One day he lured Megan over to his house. He said he would show her a puppy.

New laws were made after Megan's murder. Together, these laws are known as Megan's Law.

Megan's Law protects neighborhoods from sex offenders. Sex offenders now must register when they are released from prison. They must tell police where they live and work. They also must tell police if they move or change jobs. The police tell people in the neighborhood about the offender.

Web sites are also part of Megan's Law. These free public sites list information about known sex offenders. That way people can see if there are sex offenders in their area.

Is Bite Mark Evidence Real Proof?

There is some *controversy* about bite mark evidence. It's not always foolproof. A bite mark in something like wax is pretty clear. But human tissue has many layers. Skin can stretch or shrink. Fluids can fill in spaces. The evidence can be *subjective*. One expert can *interpret* it differently than another.

Ray Krone is a good example. A court convicted the former postal worker on bite mark evidence. One of his top front teeth stuck out. He was nicknamed the Snaggletooth Killer.

A woman had been murdered in a Phoenix bar. There were bite marks on her body. Ray Krone had a clean record. But the bite mark evidence convicted him of murder. In 1992 the court sentenced Krone to death. At a new trial in 1994, his sentence was changed to 46 years in prison.

An Innocent Man

In 2001, scientists performed DNA testing on fluid found on the victim. Computer analysis compared it to a nationwide database of DNA samples. There was a match. The results proved that Kenneth Phillips was the actual killer. Ray Krone was innocent.

In 2002 Krone was released. By then he'd been in prison for over 10 years. The government awarded him $4.4 million for the mistake. The Arizona legislature publicly apologized.

Today Ray Krone travels the world telling his story. He also works for Witness to Innocence. This organization works to ban the death penalty. It supports former death row inmates who were proven innocent. It makes the public aware of flaws in the system.

CHAPTER 2

FORENSIC BALLISTICS

DATAFILE

T I M E L I N E

August 1977

Police arrest the .44 Caliber Killer after he terrorizes New York.

October 2002

The D.C. snipers kill 10 people.

October 24, 2002

A SWAT team arrests John Muhammad and Lee Boyd Malvo.

Where is Wheaton, Maryland?

KEY TERMS

ammunition—bullets or other material fired from a weapon

ballistic fingerprinting—the process of identifying the gun used in a crime

sniper—someone who shoots people from a concealed place

striations—grooves or stripes in a spent bullet

trajectory—the path a moving object travels through space

DID YOU KNOW?

Ballistics evidence was first admitted in court in 1902. Oliver Wendell Holmes proved a certain gun was the murder weapon. Holmes was a famous Supreme Court justice.

FORENSIC BALLISTICS

Ballistics is the study of guns and bullets. Law enforcement officials call this *forensic ballistics*. *Ballistic fingerprinting* matches the gun used in a crime with bullets found at the scene. Like human fingerprints, each gun produces a unique signature.

There's a government department that covers guns. It's the Bureau of Alcohol, Tobacco, and Firearms, or ATF. The ATF's ballistics fingerprinting database is called *IBIS*. That stands for *Integrated Ballistics Information System*. It links information about guns from all over the country. Many cases have been solved with IBIS.

Panic in the City

In the summer of 1977 a killer was loose in New York City. People were scared. The killer was targeting young women and their boyfriends. Couples were killed while they were kissing in parked cars.

A ballistics expert found a connection. There had been several shootings with the same gun. It was a rather unusual handgun. It was called a Charter Arms Bulldog.

The Bulldog was a high-powered five-shot revolver. It was designed for use by *sky marshals*. In the 1970s there were a number of skyjackings. Terrorists were hijacking airplanes. Sky marshals were undercover police who worked on airplanes.

Sky marshals needed a very special gun. It needed to work well at close range.

The bullets needed to have a short *trajectory*. They couldn't go very far. The plane could crash if a bullet pierced the plane's hull. So the Charter Arms Bulldog used special *ammunition,* or bullets.

A Serial Killer at Work

Police quickly realized the shootings were the work of a serial killer. The people of New York City panicked. They were afraid to go out at night.

Newspapers began calling the shooter the .44 Caliber Killer. The term *.44 caliber* refers to a type of gun. The Charter Arms Bulldog was a .44 caliber revolver. This handgun made unusual markings on bullets. Police found spent bullets at the crime scenes. The *striations,* or grooves, helped detectives identify the Bulldog. That information eventually helped lead them to the killer.

Police arrested David Berkowitz, the .44 Caliber Killer, in August 1977. He was mentally ill. He said demons had made him commit the murders.

His nickname was Son of Sam. That name came from his neighbor, Sam Carr. Carr's barking dog bothered Berkowitz. Berkowitz shot and wounded the dog. He claimed Carr was the devil. "Son of Sam" meant he thought he was the son of the devil.

An Angry Young Man

Berkowitz was very angry about being adopted. He was born in 1953. His real parents had been having an affair. They were both married to other partners. His mother gave up her baby when he was a week old. Nathan and Pearl Berkowitz adopted him. They couldn't have children of their own.

Growing up, little David was told his mother had died in childbirth. He thought it was his fault. This made him feel very guilty. He imagined his real father murdering him to get even for her death.

As an adult he found out it was all a lie. So he wanted to stop unwanted pregnancies. That's why he attacked young women kissing in cars. His first victim was a 14-year-old girl. He tried stabbing her. But her winter coat was too thick. She struggled and got away.

After that he decided to use a gun. He went to visit an old army buddy in Houston. The friend helped him get a gun. It was the Charter Arms Bulldog.

Police arrested David Berkowitz in August 1977. By then the Son of Sam had murdered six people. He had injured seven others. He is still in prison.

The D.C. Sniper Attacks

October 2002 was a terrifying month in the Washington, D.C., area. People were being shot at random. There didn't seem to be any pattern. Victims included men, women, blacks, whites, Hispanics, and other groups. The *sniper* seemed to be invisible. It was like a ghost was doing the shooting.

The killings were happening in broad daylight. Victims were doing everyday things. Several were pumping gas. One was vacuuming her car. Another was loading groceries. One man was mowing a lawn. Then suddenly they were dead. No one ever saw the shooter.

Police were stumped. They knew one thing, though. The shootings were all done with the same gun. Ballistics proved the murder weapon was a Bushmaster XM-15. This high-powered .223 caliber rifle

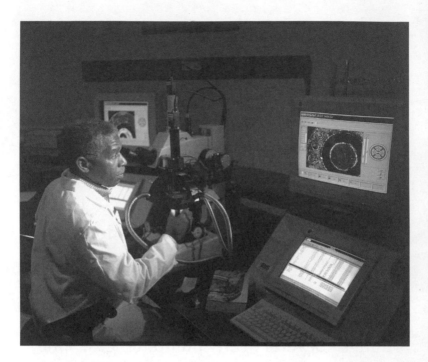

Walter Dandridge, chief forensic firearms invest-
igator on the Washington, D.C., sniper murder
case, studying grooves on a .223 slug.

is accurate from far away. It is similar to military AK-47s.

Two Men in a Dark Car

Police and media guessed the killer was a white man in his 30s. (About 80 percent of serial killers are white men.) They thought he was driving a white box truck.

They were wrong. There were actually two killers. They were black men. One was 41-year-old John Muhammad. He was an angry Gulf War veteran. The other was 17-year-old Lee Boyd Malvo. This young man was from Antigua. Muhammad had taught him how to shoot.

The killers drove a dark blue 1990 Chevy Caprice. They had rigged it for shooting. Muhammad drove. Malvo would pull the back seat out and climb into the trunk. They had filed a hole above the license plate. It was just big enough to fit the Bushmaster's barrel. Malvo shot through the hole.

A Witness Calls 911

Muhammad put a silencer on the Bushmaster. That was so witnesses wouldn't hear a loud bang. It was also easier on Malvo's ears in the trunk.

Police got the license number of the Caprice. They broadcast it on the police band. Reporters were listening. They told people to watch for a dark blue Caprice with New Jersey plates. A man saw the Caprice and called 911 on his cell phone. A SWAT team sprang into action. Police dragged Muhammad and Malvo out of the car.

The court sentenced Muhammad to death. Malvo got life in prison.

The D.C. snipers were out of business.

CHAPTER 3
COMPUTER FORENSICS

DATAFILE

T I M E L I N E

March 17, 2005

Brazilian cops arrest Valdir Paulo de Almeida after his phishing scam nets $37 million.

November 2006

Michael Fiola's employer issues a work laptop to him that nearly ruins his life.

May 15, 2008

Lori Drew is charged with cyber-bullying that led to the suicide of 13-year-old Megan Meier.

Where is Dardenne Prairie, Missouri?

KEY TERMS

computer forensics—the branch of forensics having to do with computers

cyber—having to do with computers or the Internet

firewall—software that protects a computer from malware

malware—software that harms a computer; it includes viruses, worms, and Trojans

phishing—the crime of fraud by sending out fake emails to get passwords

DID YOU KNOW?

Dennis Rader was known as the BTK Killer. Computer forensics helped convict Rader. He sent notes to police on diskettes. Computer forensics experts analyzed them. They found the names "Dennis" and "Christ Lutheran Church" in the data on the disks. That information led police to the killer.

COMPUTER FORENSICS

Michael Fiola worked for the Massachusetts government. As part of his job, he visited various companies. He used a work laptop to send reports back to his office in Boston.

In November 2006 the laptop was stolen from his car. His company issued him another one. It had been used before by another employee. The computer people at his job had set it up for Fiola.

He used the laptop for several months. Everything seemed fine. Then one day in March 2007 Fiola's boss called him into his office. Fiola was being fired. His boss said he had downloaded illegal child pornography on his work laptop.

Fiola was in shock. He didn't even know *how* to download porn. He was in his 50s and wasn't very good with computers. All he used the laptop for was work.

Forensics to the Rescue

Now all of a sudden Fiola had no income or benefits. Friends and family wouldn't talk to him. His wife stood by him. She contacted an attorney.

They hired a *computer forensics* specialist, Tami Loehrs, from Arizona. Loehrs found that the computer was crawling with *malware*. The *firewall* was turned off. So was the virus protection.

The computer had been improperly set up before it was given to Fiola. Loehrs proved that the porn images had not been downloaded by a person. They had come from the malware. The charges were dropped.

Today Fiola has a new job in Rhode Island. He says he is planning to sue his former employer "for destroying our lives."

Computer Criminals

Computers are a favorite tool of criminals today. Computer crime comes in many forms. Two big types of computer crime are fraud and identity theft.

Computer forensics experts help catch these criminals. As *cyber* detectives, they follow the criminals' electronic data trail. They use special forensics software like EnCase.

Phishing scams are a big part of the identity theft problem. A phishing scam involves sending out phony emails. These seem to come from a trusted source.

Common phishing scams appear to come from PayPal, eBay, or banks.

Victims think the email is about their account. Often it will prey on their fears. The subject line will say something like "Log in to restore access to your account." That can scare people. So they click on the link. It takes them to a Web site. They Web site asks for their username and password. Everything looks like a real site, such as PayPal.

But it's not. The emails are really from criminals. They just need your username and password. Then they can go to your real account. Once there, they can steal all your money.

Brazilian Phishing Kingpin Arrested

Valdir Paulo de Almeida of Brazil was one cyber criminal. He was the kingpin of a group of fraudsters.

His gang sent out fake banking emails. Every day they sent more than three million emails. The emails contained a type of malware called a Trojan horse. A Trojan horse gets passwords by recording keystrokes. Almeida's gang stole money from thousands of people.

In March 2005 Almeida was arrested.

Luckily, prison inmates are not allowed to use computers.

A Tragic Case of Cyber-Bullying

Megan Meier was a young girl who lived in Missouri. She hanged herself in her closet when she was almost 14. It was all because of a boy.

She had met 16-year-old Josh Evans on MySpace. Well, she hadn't actually *met* him, at least not in person. They had been talking for several months on MySpace. Josh was a good-looking

Lori Drew and her daughter leave the U.S. Federal Courthouse in Los Angeles.

guy. He had seemed so sweet in the beginning.

But all of a sudden he turned nasty. He said Megan wasn't very nice to her friends. Then he got really mean. He told her the world would be better off without her.

Megan sent one last message to Josh. She said he was the kind of boy a girl would kill herself over. Then she went upstairs and hanged herself.

Only it turned out Josh Evans didn't really exist. The messages were actually just a mean prank. They were the work of two women, Lori Drew and Ashley Grills. Lori Drew was the mother of a neighbor girl. Ashley Grills, 18, worked for Lori. Lori's daughter was the same age as Megan.

A Friendship Gone Bad

Megan used to be friends with Lori's daughter. But it was an on-again, off-again friendship. The girls had had a falling out. Lori wanted to find out what Megan was saying about her daughter on MySpace.

Lori, her daughter, and Ashley cooked up the Josh Evans idea. They found pictures of a good-looking boy. They set up a fake MySpace account under the name Josh Evans. They were pretending to be Josh to gain Megan's confidence. Then they pounced. Their meanness crushed poor Megan.

This was a landmark case of cyber-bullying. But as a crime, it didn't fit neatly into any categories. The FBI investigated for over a year. Computer forensics experts pieced everything together. They determined there was no crime to prosecute. During that time Megan's parents kept quiet about the case. The FBI had told them not to talk. The FBI was investigating the Drews. They didn't want the Drews to know.

After the FBI said there was no crime the Meiers went public. They told reporters the whole story. After that, there was a media frenzy.

Finally Lori Drew was charged with several computer-related crimes. The trial took place in Los Angeles. That's where MySpace is located. The court convicted Lori. In July 2009 a judge threw out her conviction.

CHAPTER 4

FACIAL RECONSTRUCTION

DATAFILE

T I M E L I N E

1960s

Mikhail Gerasimov develops facial reconstruction technique.

May 21, 1989

The John List episode of *America's Most Wanted* airs.

June 1, 1989

Police arrest List 18 years after he murdered his family.

Where is Westfield, New Jersey?

K E Y   T E R M S

age progression—modifying a photo or bust to show how a person would have aged

anthropologist—a scientist who studies the origins of human beings

bust—a sculpture of a person's head and shoulders

facial reconstruction—a drawing or sculpture showing what a person's face would look like

hominids—early ancestors of human beings

DID YOU KNOW?

Karen Taylor is a real-life forensic artist. Her facial reconstructions help solve crimes. Karen's work also appears on the TV show *CSI*. Her hands can be seen on the show. They are working on clay busts.

FACIAL RECONSTRUCTION

Facial reconstruction is a tool used to help solve crimes. It is used when an unidentified skeleton has been found. It can help identify the body. It is also used in *age progressions*. They show what a missing person would look like years later.

Facial reconstruction is just one of many forensic tools. It is different in one important way. It cannot be used as evidence in court. This is because it is subjective. The artist's imagination comes into play. He or she decides what kind of lips, ears, hair, and eyes to add. So it is not as strong as DNA evidence, for example. But facial reconstruction can still be quite useful.

There are several kinds of facial reconstruction. They can be 2-D or 3-D. A drawing would be 2-D, or two-dimensional. A sketch artist measures the skull. Then the artist makes a drawing of the victim's face.

A skilled artist can make the drawing look like the victim. It will not look *exactly* like the person, however. The artist doesn't know how the lips or eyes were shaped. But a skull gives many clues to a trained forensic artist.

Sculptures that Solve Crimes

Three-dimensional, or 3-D, reconstructions can be handmade sculptures. Artists make these *busts* using clay or similar materials.

The artist starts with either the actual skull or a copy of it. Then the artist adds layers of clay for the muscles and skin.

These 3-D reconstructions can also be created on a computer. This is known as a *digital* facial reconstruction. Sometimes clay and digital are used together. First a clay bust is photographed. The digital photo is then put into a computer. Hair and other features are added to the picture using photo software.

Russian scientist Mikhail Gerasimov was an *anthropologist*. He made sculptures showing what early humans' faces probably looked like. He based them on the skulls of extinct *hominids*. Then in the 1960s, his students developed a new way to use the technique. They used it to help solve crimes. They were among the first to make forensic facial reconstructions.

Caught after 18 Years in Hiding

John Emil List was a New Jersey Sunday school teacher. In November 1971, he shot and killed his wife, mother, and three kids. First, List shot his wife in the back of the head. She slumped over the kitchen table. Then he went upstairs and shot his mother. He calmly cleaned up and had lunch. His three children came home from school one by one. As they came in, he shot them too.

The family lived in a run-down mansion. After the murders, List placed the bodies on sleeping bags. He laid them out neatly in the mansion's ballroom. His mother was too heavy to move. He left her body upstairs. She had an apartment up there.

He called the kids' schools. He wrote a letter to the church pastor. He also called

After 18 years as a fugitive, an artist for the television show *America's Most Wanted* created a clay bust of an aging John List. A tipster called the show after recognizing his former neighbor. John List (shown here) was arrested twelve days later.

other people, including his work. He told everybody his mother was very ill. He said the family would be out of town for a while. He put a hold on mail delivery. He canceled the newspaper.

Then he drove to the airport. He parked his car there and left town. The bodies weren't found until nearly a month later. By then John List was long gone. Nearly 18 years passed before police found him.

America's Most Wanted Investigates

John Walsh was very interested in the case. He hosts the popular Fox TV show *America's Most Wanted*. The List case was the oldest unsolved case ever featured on the show.

Forensic facial reconstruction played a big role in List's capture. *America's Most Wanted* had an artist make a clay bust. It showed what John List would look like after 18 years.

Artist Frank Bender made the sculpture. He looked at photos of List's parents. That helped him see how List would age. He gave the bust a receding hairline and sagging cheeks.

Bender also had help from a forensic psychologist. The psychologist said List would want to seem more important than he was. He'd want to appear wise and professional. So Bender added square glasses to the bust. The result looked amazingly like John List, 18 years older.

Brilliant Detective Work

John Walsh called Bender's sculpture "brilliant detective work." He kept the bust in an honored spot in his office for many years.

The show about John List's unsolved case first aired on May 21, 1989. The clay bust made by Frank Bender was shown. Walsh asked people to call if they knew someone who looked similar. Police set up a hotline. They got more than 250 tips. One was from someone in Denver. The caller said the bust looked a lot like a former neighbor.

Police arrested John List twelve days later. He had remarried and moved to Denver. Then he moved to Virginia. Police took List back to New Jersey to stand trial. The court sentenced him to five life terms.

In 2008 he died in prison of pneumonia. He was 82.

CHAPTER 5

FINGERPRINTING

DATAFILE

T I M E L I N E

May 23, 1905

The Stratton brothers are hanged in London for robbery and double murder.

July 1999

The FBI's IAFIS fingerprint database goes into operation.

May 6, 2004

The FBI mistakenly arrests Brandon Mayfield.

Where is Portland, Oregon?

KEY TERMS

biometrics—using physical characteristics to identify people, such as fingerprints or DNA

friction ridges—raised skin lines that make up a fingerprint

latent print—a hidden or invisible fingerprint

patent print—a visible fingerprint

plastic print—a fingerprint made in something that holds an impression, such as candle wax or putty

DID YOU KNOW?

John Doe and *Jane Doe* are names given to unidentified bodies. These are people who died with no identification. A group called the Doe Network helps find out who these people were. Doe Network volunteers often use fingerprints to match missing persons with unidentified bodies.

FINGERPRINTING

Fingerprints are a very helpful crime-solving tool. There are billions of people on Earth. No two people have exactly the same prints. Even identical twins have different fingerprints.

Fingerprints have long been used to establish identity. In the 7th century Arab merchants used them in sales contracts. In the early 1900s investigators began using fingerprints to solve crimes.

The first time fingerprints were used to solve a major case was in 1905. Many think that was the case that launched forensic science.

1905 London Murders

A sensational double murder occurred in London. Thomas and Ann Farrow ran a small art supply store. Thomas was 71. Ann was 65. One day, two thugs robbed the store. They beat the Farrows to death.

Brothers Alfred and Albert Stratton wore black masks while committing the crime. The case became known as the Mask Murders. Scotland Yard detectives fingerprinted both men. Scotland Yard is United Kingdom's version of the FBI.

Alfred Stratton had left a clear thumbprint on the cash box. It was enough to convict both brothers. On May 23, 1905, the Strattons were hanged for murder.

FBI Fingerprint Database

Scotland Yard had only a few sets of prints in its files back then. A fingerprint expert had to compare each print by hand. Today computers make the task much faster and easier. And it's possible to store millions of fingerprint sets on computers.

The FBI's fingerprint database is called *IAFIS*. That stands for *Integrated Automated Fingerprint Identification System*. This database covers local, state, and federal law enforcement agencies.

It includes fingerprints of anyone arrested. Fingerprints of military personnel are in there, too. Other sources of prints include background checks and immigration records. Altogether, IAFIS holds more than 55 million sets of fingerprints. It's the largest *biometrics* database in the world.

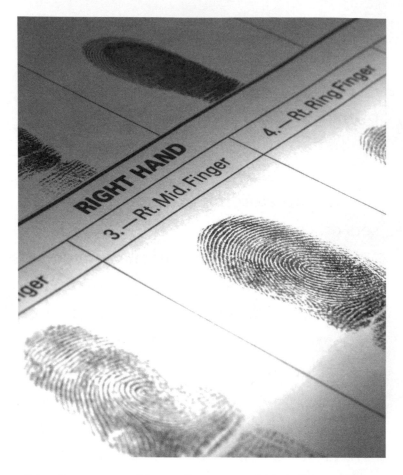

LiveScan provides clearer prints than those on paper as seen in this photograph. LiveScan eliminates smudging or having too much or too little ink.

Ways to Record Prints

Police traditionally used an inkpad to record a person's fingerprints. They rolled the person's inked fingers onto a white card. This results in a complete set of prints. Then the police scanned the prints and added them to the database.

Today there's an inkless device called LiveScan. It electronically transmits fingerprints to the Department of Justice. People applying for certain types of licenses have to get LiveScan fingerprints.

LiveScan prints also become part of the IAFIS database. The LiveScan device provides clearer prints than ink on paper. It eliminates problems like smudging or having too much or too little ink.

Types of Fingerprints

There are several types of fingerprints. A *latent print* is hidden or invisible. This type of print may be found on surfaces like glass. Latent prints require special powder or other means to record the print. A *patent print* is visible. Bloody fingerprints are patent prints. A *plastic print* is found in material that holds an impression. Plastic prints can be found in candle wax or putty.

Friction ridges are the curving lines on skin that make up fingerprints. Our fingers naturally sweat a little bit. That moisture gets on the friction ridges. That's how fingerprints are created.

The friction ridges make up various patterns. These include arches, loops, and whorls. They come together in different combinations. Fingerprints are compared at various points. A good match contains many similar points.

Scientists can also analyze the oily residue that creates prints. This can tell a forensics expert if the person is a smoker or does drugs.

The Brandon Mayfield Case

Brandon Mayfield is a lawyer in Portland, Oregon. His wife, Mona, is from Egypt. Brandon converted to Islam when they got married. After the attacks of September 11, 2001, he was concerned for his family's safety. Many people had become hostile to people of Islamic faith.

On May 6, 2004, the FBI arrested Mayfield. Police would not tell him why they were arresting him. He was not allowed to see his family for two weeks. His wife was not told where her husband was being held.

Finally the FBI released information to the public. Mayfield's family saw it on the news. The FBI claimed he was involved in a terrible train bombing in Madrid, Spain.

FORENSICS

This terrorist act killed 191 people. In addition, it wounded more than 1,800 people.

The FBI said Mayfield's fingerprints were on bomb parts found in the wreckage. But he had not been outside the United States for 11 years. He couldn't have been in Spain. Spanish authorities said the prints belonged to an Algerian national, Ouhnane Daoud.

The U.S. government formally apologized to Mayfield after the incident. Later a court awarded him $2 million in a settlement.

GLOSSARY

age progression—modifying a photo or bust to show how a person would have aged

ammunition—bullets or other material fired from a weapon

anthropologist—a scientist who studies the origins of human beings

ballistic fingerprinting –the process of identifying the gun used in a crime

biometrics—using physical characteristics to identify people, such as fingerprints or DNA

bust—a sculpture of a person's head and shoulders

computer forensics—the branch of forensics having to do with computers

controversy—an issue people disagree on

cyber—having to do with computers or the Internet

facial reconstruction—a drawing or sculpture showing what a person's face would look like

GLOSSARY

firewall—software that protects a computer from malware

friction ridges—raised skin lines that make up a fingerprint

hominids—early ancestors of human beings

interpret—to explain the meaning of something

latent print—a hidden or invisible fingerprint

malware—software that harms a computer; it includes viruses, worms, and Trojans

odontology—the study of teeth and gums

orthodontist—a type of dentist who fixes crooked teeth

patent print—a visible fingerprint

phishing—the crime of fraud by sending out fake emails to get passwords

plastic print—a fingerprint made in something that holds an impression, such as candle wax or putty

sniper—someone who shoots people from a concealed place

striations—grooves or stripes in a spent bullet

subjective—based on opinion rather than fact

trajectory—the path a moving object travels through space

INDEX

INDEX